WAR MACHINES

TANKS

by
David West

CRABTREE
PUBLISHING COMPANY
WWW.CRABTREEBOOKS.COM

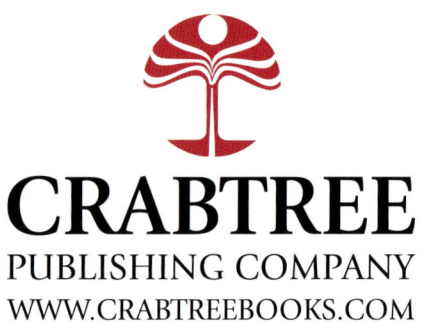

CRABTREE
PUBLISHING COMPANY
WWW.CRABTREEBOOKS.COM

Author and designer: David West

Illustrator: David West

Editorial director: Kathy Middleton

Editor: Ellen Rodger

Proofreader: Melissa Boyce

Production coordinator and Prepress technician: Ken Wright

Print coordinator: Katherine Berti

Library and Archives Canada Cataloguing in Publication

Title: Tanks / David West.
Names: West, David, 1956- author.
Description: Series statement: War machines | Includes index.
Identifiers: Canadiana (print) 20190099410 |
    Canadiana (ebook) 20190099429 |
    ISBN 9780778766841 (softcover) |
    ISBN 9780778766698 (hardcover) |
    ISBN 9781427124111 (HTML)
Subjects: LCSH: Tanks—Juvenile literature.
Classification: LCC UG446.5 .W47 2019 |
    DDC j358.1/883—dc23

Library of Congress Cataloging-in-Publication Data

Names: West, David, 1956- author.
Title: Tanks / David West.
Description: New York : Crabtree Publishing Company, [2019]
    Series: War machines | Includes index. |
    Audience: Grades 7-8. | Audience: Ages 10-14 and up. |
Identifiers: LCCN 2019014265 (print) |
    LCCN 2019017527 (ebook) |
    ISBN 9781427124111 (Electronic) |
    ISBN 9780778766698 (hardcover) |
    ISBN 9780778766841 (pbk.)
Subjects: LCSH: Tanks--Juvenile literature.
Classification: LCC UG446.5 (ebook) |
    LCC UG446.5 .W42843 2019 (print) | DDC 358.1/883--dc23
LC record available at https://lccn.loc.gov/2019014265

Crabtree Publishing Company
www.crabtreebooks.com   1-800-387-7650

Published by Crabtree Publishing Company in 2020

All rights reserved. No part of this publication may be reproduced, stored in a retrieval system or be transmitted in any form or by any means, electronic, mechanical, photocopying, recording, or otherwise, without the prior written permission of copyright owner.

Copyright © 2019 David West Children's Books
Project development, design, and concept:
David West Children's Books

Printed in the U.S.A./072019/CG20190501

Published in Canada
Crabtree Publishing
616 Welland Ave.
St. Catharines, ON
L2M 5V6

Published in the United States
Crabtree Publishing
PMB 59051, 350 Fifth Ave.
59th Floor,
New York, NY

Contents

Armored Tanks 4
The First Tanks 6
Tanks Take Shape 8
Light Tanks 10
Infantry Tanks 12
Hobart's Funnies 14
Heavy Tanks 16
Tank Destroyers 18
Main Battle Tanks 20
Tankettes 22
Amphibious Tanks 24
Infantry Fighting Vehicles 26
Modern MBTs 28

Tank Specs
More information about the tanks 30
Glossary 31
Index 32

Armored Tanks

A tank is an armored fighting vehicle with heavy firepower, strong armor, and a powerful engine. Using a geared wheel, the engine drives the tank along linked tracks called caterpillar tracks. These provide it with its own roadway, spreading its weight over a large surface. They allow the tank to travel over rough terrain where a wheeled vehicle would become bogged down or stuck.

When tanks began to be used by modern armies, a new type of combat emerged. It used armored killing machines that could roll over barbed wire and withstand bullets, all while shooting heavy guns at the enemy. Tanks soon became a key part of coordinated combat, where areas of the military worked together to achieve a goal. Today, the latest tanks are called main battle tanks (MBTs). They have armor that reacts to the impact of weapons to reduce damage, as well as laser range finders and heat-sensing cameras that can track targets up to a range of 6.1 miles (9.8 km) away.

South Korean K2 Black Panther main battle tanks on maneuvers.

World War I
1914–1918
France

The First Tanks

The first tanks were used by the British Army on the European battlefields of the **Western Front** during **World War I** (WWI). Tanks could go where no humans dared—across the dangerous territory between enemy trenches known as **no-man's land**.

The first tanks, called the Mark I, were built in total secrecy. The manufacturers told their workforce that they were building tanks to hold water, and the name stuck. These first tanks were slow and clumsy and

During the Battle of Cambrai in France, two British Mark IV tanks break through German lines on November 20, 1917. Along with **infantry**, more than 400 tanks made it through 6 miles (9 km) of enemy-held territory. The territory was recaptured in a counterattack.

many broke down. They had a shell-firing cannon on each side and three machine guns. A crew of eight operated in stifling heat while breathing in poisonous engine fumes. The first Mark I tanks appeared on the battlefield on September 15, 1916, during the **Battle of the Somme**.

By 1918, small, light tanks called Whippets were used. They had a crew of three armed with machine guns.

After the War
1918–1930
France

Tanks Take Shape

During the Second Battle of the Marne, towards the end of WWI in 1918, the French Army **deployed** a new small, light tank. It had its engine in the rear and a rotating turret. It was called a Renault FT, and it influenced tank design worldwide.

At the same time, the French were also designing a super-heavy tank called the Char 2C. It was the largest tank ever made, but was not produced until after the war in 1921. The armor was 1.8 inches

A French Renault FT (1) and a Char 2C (2) roll through a French village in 1923. The Renault FT's design influenced many later tanks. The crew compartment was in the front and the engine was in the back, with a revolving turret. This became standard on all tanks.

(45 mm) thick and it had a 75 mm cannon in its turret. There were also four machine guns, one of which was mounted in a turret at the rear. A crew of 12 entered the tank through a door in the side of the main body. Char 2Cs stayed operational until 1940 but were never used in war.

The Renault FT was exported to many countries and served in several wars, including the **Spanish Civil War** (1936–1939). Various types were made by countries such as Russia and Italy. The Italian Fiat 3000 is shown here.

9

Spanish Civil War
1936–1939
Spain

Light Tanks

By the 1930s, between World War I and **World War II** (WWII), European companies and armies were building light tanks. Many were used by both sides during the Spanish Civil War (1936–1939).

The Spanish Civil War pitted the Republican government against the Nationalists. The Republicans were supported by the **Soviet Union**, Mexico, and international volunteers. The Nationalists were supported by Nazi Germany, **Fascist** Italy, and Portugal.

Spanish Republican Army T-26 (1) and BT-5 (2) tanks lead a convoy of armored vehicles to the front during the Spanish Civil War. These Soviet-made tanks were operated by Soviet volunteers.

In 1937, Republican troops defeated the Nationalists with the help of Soviet-supplied tanks in the **Battle of Guadalajara**. Many of the tanks during this period were armed only with machine guns. The Republicans produced some of their own light tanks at a factory that was later captured by the Nationalists. Nationalist forces used German Panzer tanks and captured T-26 tanks.

The German Panzer II was a light tank produced in the 1930s and used by Spain's Nationalist forces. It had a 20 mm autocannon.

11

World War II
1939–1945
North Africa

Infantry Tanks

Infantry tanks were developed by the British and French between WWI and WWII. They were designed to support the infantry in an attack. Once infantry tanks helped break through enemy lines, cruiser tanks were then used for their higher speed and longer range.

Infantry tanks such as the British Matilda II, armed with a 40 mm cannon, were often heavily armored. This cost them speed. These tanks performed well at the beginning of the war, but they were soon

Infantry of the British Eighth Army advance past a Matilda II infantry tank (1) during Operation Crusader in North Africa, November 18–December 30, 1941. A Panzer III (2) and IV (3) are shown destroyed.

outgunned by German tanks such as the Panzer IV. Eventually they were replaced by medium and heavy tanks, such as the American Sherman and the British Churchill heavy infantry tank.

Cruiser tanks (also known as cavalry tanks), like this Crusader I, were fast and mobile. Early cruisers were only lightly armored and armed to save weight. Later cruisers had bigger and heavier 75 mm cannons.

World War II
1939–1945
Europe

Hobart's Funnies

Hobart's Funnies were tanks used during WWII. They were modified to help them make their way through soft sand during the beach landings of **D-Day** in 1944. They were named after Major General Percy Hobart, the British tank genius who helped create them.

As D-Day approached, Britain was concerned about the tank's shortcomings in maneuvering over tough terrain. In 1943, Hobart was given command of the British Army's 79th Armored Division. His division

An adapted AVRE (Assault Vehicle Royal Engineers) Churchill tank carries and places a bridge to replace one destroyed in action. The bridge was used to ferry troops and equipment across a river.

developed a "zoo" of unique armored fighting vehicles and tanks to ensure they would not be bogged down and made useless during the **Allied** invasion. The tanks included a Crocodile flamethrower and a mine-clearing Crab flail tank. Their funny design brought about the nickname Hobart's Funnies.

Hobart's Funnies and other modified tanks, such as this Sherman with a dozer attachment, helped make the invasion a success.

World War II
1939–1945
Soviet Union

Heavy Tanks

As tank-on-tank combat increased during WWII, tank technology evolved and improved. More heavily armored tanks with powerful antitank guns appeared on the battlefield. These heavy tanks were used to break through enemy defenses and antitank units.

Heavy tanks were more expensive to produce, so there were fewer of them on the battlefield. Only around 1,350 German Tiger I tanks were produced, and only 492 of the later Tiger II. By comparison, the Soviets

The **Battle of Kursk** in 1943 was one of the largest tank battles of WWII. Here, German infantry advance using Tiger I heavy tanks (1), while smoke billows from a burning Soviet T-34 medium tank (2).

manufactured around 80,000 T-34s, and Americans built 49,000 M4 Sherman medium tanks. These heavy tanks were often unreliable and prone to track failures and breakdowns. They used a lot of fuel to operate, which gave them a limited range.

Later in the war, the Allies used heavy tanks such as the U.S. M26 Pershing with a 90 mm gun, shown here, and the Soviet IS tank which carried a 122 mm gun. The Allies' last heavy tanks were introduced just after the war to counter the Soviet IS series. These included the U.S. M103 heavy tank, the British FV214 Conqueror, and the French ARL 44.

World War II
1939–1945
Russia

Tank Destroyers

Tank destroyers, sometimes called tank hunters, first appeared during WWII. Groups of these motorized artillery destroyers were designed to take on enemy tanks and other armored fighting vehicles.

Some were simple designs, such as the Marder III. It was an antitank gun mounted on a tracked vehicle to give it mobility. Others, such as the Jagdpanzer 38, did not have a turret. This allowed more room inside to house crew and extra ammunition. It also gave it a lower

The crew of a German Jagdpanzer 38 tries to repair the engine of their tank destroyer in the freezing cold of winter on the **Eastern Front**. A kubelwagen, or "tub car," light military vehicle attempts to pass the blocked track.

profile than a tank. The sloped sides and thicker armor made the Jagdpanzer 38 a difficult target to knock out. It was based on a modified Czechoslovakian-designed Panzer 38 frame and machinery, and carried a powerful 75 mm gun.

Since WWII, gun-armed tank destroyers have become lightly armored antitank guided missile (ATGM) carriers. This gun-armed Italian B1 Centauro wheeled vehicle carries a 105 mm gun.

19

1973 Arab-Israeli War
October 6–25, 1973
Middle East

Main Battle Tanks

The main battle tank (MBT), sometimes called the universal tank, appeared at the end of WWII. MBTs had the armor protection of a heavy tank, mobility of a light tank, and firepower of a super-heavy tank.

The British Centurion was the first MBT. Originally designed as a cruiser tank, its powerful engine allowed it to carry heavier armor without loss of speed. The addition of an 84 mm gun gave the tank a big advantage over other tanks of the era. The MBTs were the first multipurpose tanks of the **Cold War**—an era of heightened military tensions. By the

During the **1973 Arab-Israeli War**, two Israeli Centurion main battle tanks (1) advance past a smoking, knocked-out Syrian T-62 tank (2).

1960s, antitank rounds could penetrate 3 feet (1 m) of steel. This led to designs of composite armor, where layers of different material were sandwiched between inner and outer steel. The Soviet T-64 MBT had layers of glass reinforced plastic between steel. Glass has good "stopping power." British Chobham armor included ceramics in its layers.

The United States and the Soviet Union produced their first MBTs during the early 1960s.

Somali Civil War
1991–present
Somalia

Tankettes

Tankettes were tank-like fighting vehicles. They were much smaller than light tanks and similar in size to cars. Many didn't have turrets and some had such a low profile that the crew had to lie down inside. The main weapons on tankettes were machine guns or, occasionally, a 20 mm autocannon.

Tankettes were mainly used for scouting and supporting infantry. They were built by many countries between the 1920s and 1940s. Some were

A Wiesel Armored Weapons Carrier armed with an antitank guided missile system (1) and a second armed with an autocannon (2) emerge from a CH-53 Sea Stallion helicopter. This was part of the United Nations mission in the **Somali Civil War**.

used in combat during WWII. Their light armor made them vulnerable to antitank weapons, which led armies to abandon their use. Their role was taken over by armored cars. The 1990s saw the tankette return to the German Army as the Wiesel Armored Weapons Carrier (AWC). It was designed to provide **reconnaissance** for airborne paratroopers, or parachute troops.

The most common Italian armored fighting vehicle during WWII was the Carro Veloce CV-35 tankette. It was a two-man vehicle armed with two machine guns.

Vietnam War
1955–1975
Vietnam

Amphibious Tanks

After WWI, a few countries experimented with tanks that could swim across large bodies of water such as rivers and lakes. The Soviet Union was one of the few countries that produced light **amphibious** tanks during WWII. These were the T-37A and T-38.

During the Normandy beach landings in 1944, M4 Sherman medium tanks were made amphibious by attaching a rubberized canvas screen. This provided additional buoyancy. Propellers were added to drive the

North Vietnamese Army infantry ride on the back of Soviet-made PT-76 amphibious light tanks as they cross a river during the Vietnam War.

engine. Many of these sank due to rough conditions. Those that made it ashore provided fire support in the first hours of the invasion. After the war, the Soviet Army continued with its development of light amphibious tanks. The PT-76 saw action in various wars, including the **Vietnam War**.

The United States continued to develop tracked landing vehicles such as this LVT-5. It was armed with a howitzer and was used during the Vietnam War.

First Gulf War
1990–1991
Middle East

Infantry Fighting Vehicles

Infantry fighting vehicles (IFVs) are armored fighting vehicles. They are designed to be faster than tanks. IFVs are equipped with an autocannon and often have antitank missiles. Their main job is to support the infantry and protect it from small arms and artillery fire.

Most IFVs provide protection for troops. Infantry units with armored IFVs could also eliminate enemy antitank weapons. By 1982, IFVs were used by 30 national armies. American IFVs, such as the Bradley M2A2s, had

A British FV510 Warrior Infantry Fighting Vehicle (1) stops near a burning U.S. Bradley IFV (2) during Operation Desert Storm. Both vehicles entered service during the 1980s.

additional armor to protect against shrapnel and higher-caliber ammunition. The protection added weight to the IFV but made it better able to withstand tank rounds. Cannon and armor weights have also increased over time.

In 1956, the German Army built the first IFV. It was the SPz 12-3, an armored personnel carrier (APC) with a turret-mounted 20 mm autocannon that enabled it to engage with other armored vehicles. Many countries' armies did the same by modifying their existing APCs. The Soviet Army's first IFV, the BMP-1 (right), entered service in 1966.

Iraq War
2003–2011
Iraq

Modern MBTs

Modern main battle tanks are known as third-generation MBTs. They have composite armor and computerized fire control. This allows them to fire while moving. The very latest, or "next-generation" MBTs are still in the early stages of development.

Many armies around the world were producing third-generation MBTs by the 1980s. Weighing almost 68 tons (62 metric tons), the M1 Abrams is one of the heaviest MBTs in service. The superior technology of the M1,

During the **Iraq War,** a U.S. M1 Abrams MBT (1) advances past burning Iraqi T-72 MBTs (2). The Soviet-made T-72s were second-generation MBTs, and no match for the third- generation M1s and Challengers of the coalition forces.

along with the British Challenger 2, proved unbeatable against second-generation MBTs during the **Invasion of Iraq**. MBT main guns are generally between 90 and 130 mm caliber. They fire armor-piercing rounds using range finders and thermal sights that show targets that are invisible to the naked eye.

Third-generation main battle tanks, such as this Chinese ZTZ-99A, use reactive armor that explodes when hit by an enemy missile, preventing damage to the tank.

Tank Specs

More information about the tanks in this book

Mark IV
Crew: 8
Weapons: Two 57 mm guns
Speed: 4 mph (6.4 kph)

Char 2C
Crew: 12
Weapons: 75 mm gun
Speed: 7.5 mph (12 kph)

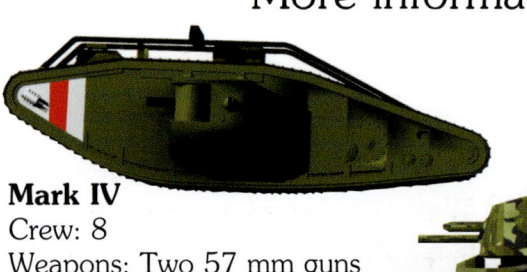

Renault FT
Crew: 2
Weapons: 37 mm gun
Speed: 9.3 mph (15 kph)

T-26
Crew: 3
Weapons: 45 mm gun
Speed: 19 mph (31 kph)

BT-5
Crew: 3
Weapons: 45 mm gun
Speed: 45 mph (72 kph)

Matilda II
Crew: 4
Weapons: 40 mm gun
Speed: 16 mph (26 kph)

Tiger I
Crew: 5
Weapons: 88 mm gun
Speed: 25 mph (40 kph)

T-34
Crew: 4
Weapons: 76.2 mm gun
Speed: 33 mph (53 kph)

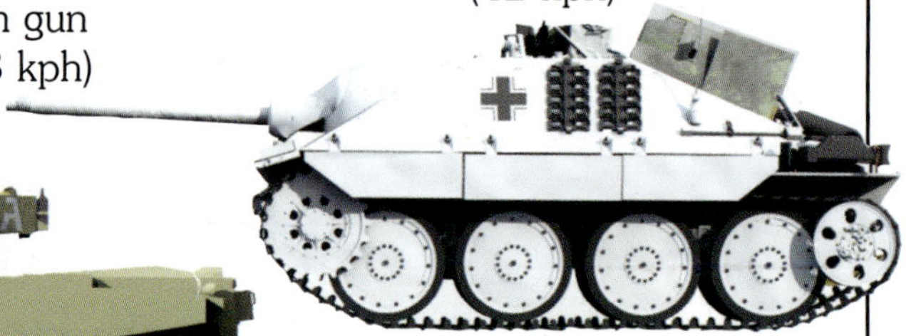

Jagdpanzer 38
Crew: 4
Weapons: 75 mm gun
Speed: 26 mph (42 kph)

FV510 Warrior
Crew: 3
Weapons: 30 mm cannon
Speed: 46 mph (75 kph)

Centurion
Crew: 4
Weapons: 105 mm gun
Speed: 22 mph (35 kph)

Bradley IFV
Crew: 3
Weapons: 25 mm gun and missiles
Speed: 35 mph (56 kph)

PT-76
Crew: 3
Weapons: 76.2 mm gun
Speed: 27 mph (44 kph)

Wiesel AWC
Crew: 2
Weapons: 25 mm cannon or missiles
Speed: 43 mph (70 kph)

M1 Abrams
Crew: 4
Weapons: 120 mm gun
Speed: 45 mph (72 kph)

Glossary

1973 Arab-Israeli War (October 6–25, 1973) A war fought by a coalition of Arab states led by Egypt and Syria against Israel

Allied The nations that fought against Nazi Germany and the Axis powers during World War II

amphibious Able to travel on land and water

Battle of Guadalajara (March 8–23, 1937) A battle of the Spanish Civil War where the People's Republican Army defeated Nationalist forces attempting to encircle Madrid

Battle of Kursk A WWII battle between Nazi Germany and Soviet troops near the city of Kursk in the Soviet Union

Battle of the Somme A WWI battle between Great Britain, its empire, and allies against the German Empire, near the River Somme in France. It was one of the largest battles of the war.

Cold War (1947–1991) The name of the politically hostile relationship between the United States and the Soviet Union after World War II

D-Day The Allied forces' invasion of France on June 6, 1944, during WWII

deployed To spread troops out in readiness for battle

Eastern Front A front line of conflict during World War II (1939–1945), between the Allies and Nazi Germany in eastern Europe

Fascist Authoritarian, right-wing person, group, or government that is typically in favor of strong control over society

infantry Soldiers or military units that typically fight on foot

Invasion of Iraq The first stage of the Iraq War in 2003 in which forces from the United States, the United Kingdom, Australia, and Poland invaded Iraq

Iraq War An armed conflict that began in 2003 with the invasion of Iraq and ended in 2011

no-man's land Unoccupied land between two opposing front lines

reconnaissance A search made by military forces of an area to get information about enemy positions, numbers, and equipment

Somali Civil War (1991–present) An ongoing war in the southeast African country of Somalia that grew out of resistance to military rule and has led to numerous changes in government and hundreds of thousands of deaths and displacements of people

Soviet Union (1922–1991) A former union of states in Eastern Europe and Asia

Spanish Civil War (1936–1939) A war between forces of the Republicans and groups from other countries that supported the Spanish democratic government, and the Nationalists, a number of different groups, including fascists, supported by Nazi Germany

Vietnam War (1955–1975) A conflict between North Vietnam and its allies, China and the Soviet Union, and South Vietnam and its allies, the United States, South Korea, Australia, and the Philippines

Western Front The main area of conflict during WWI. It stretched from the North Sea to the border of Switzerland.

World War I (1914–1918) An international conflict fought mainly in Europe and the Middle East, between the Central powers, including Austria-Hungary, Germany, and the Ottoman Empire, and the Allies, including the United Kingdom, Canada, Australia, and later, the United States

World War II (1939–1945) An international conflict fought in Europe, Asia, and Africa, between the Axis powers, including Germany, Italy, and Japan, and the Allies, including the United Kingdom, France, Canada, Australia, and in 1941, the United States

Index

autocannon 23, 26, 27

B1 Centauro 19
Battle of Cambrai 7
Battle of Guadalajara 11
Battle of Kursk 17
Battle of the Somme 7
BMP-1 27
Bradley IFV 27, 30
BT-5 11, 30

Carro Veloce CV-35 23
Centurion 21, 30
Challenger 29
Char 2C 8, 9, 30
Cold War 20, 21
composite armor 21, 28
cruiser tanks 12, 13
Crusader I 13

Fiat 3000 9
First Gulf War 26
FV214 Conqueror 17
FV510 Warrior 27, 30

Iraq War 28
IS tank 17

Jagdpanzer 38 19, 30

K2 Black Panther 5

LVT-5 25

M-60 Patton 21

M1 Abrams 20, 30
M4 Sherman 13, 15, 17, 24
M26 Pershing 17
M103 17
Marder III 18
Mark I 6, 7
Mark IV 7, 30
Mark V 7
Matilda II 13, 30

Panzer II 11
Panzer IV 13
Panzer 38 19
PT-76 25, 30

radar 5
range finder 5
reactive armor 29
Renault FT 9, 10, 30

Second Battle of the Marne 8
Somali Civil War 23
Spanish Civil War 9, 11

T-26 11, 30
T-34 17, 30
T-37 24
T-62 21
T-64 21
T-72 29
Tiger I 17, 30
Tiger II 16

Vietnam War 25

Whippet 7, 10
Wiesel AWC 23, 30
World War I 6, 8, 10, 24
World War II 11, 12, 14, 16, 17, 18, 19, 20, 23

ZTZ-99A 29

NOV 2019

UNION COUNTY PUBLIC LIBRARY
316 E. Windsor St., Monroe, NC 28112